Ketogenic Diet for Women After 50

A practical guide to develop the right mindset and avoid common mistakes, with a bonus of 42 recipes

Dana Roberts

Dana Roberts

© Copyright 2020 by Dana Roberts - All rights reserved.

The following Book is reproduced below with the goal of providing information that is as accurate and reliable as possible. Regardless, purchasing this Book can be seen as consent to the fact that both the publisher and the author of this book are in no way experts on the topics discussed within and that any recommendations or suggestions that are made herein are for entertainment purposes only. Professionals should be consulted as needed prior to undertaking any of the action endorsed herein.

This declaration is deemed fair and valid by both the American Bar Association and the Committee of Publishers Association and is legally binding throughout the United States.

Furthermore, the transmission, duplication, or reproduction of any of the following work including specific information will be considered an illegal act irrespective of if it is done electronically or in print. This extends to creating a secondary or tertiary copy of the work or a recorded copy and is only allowed with the express written consent from the Publisher. All additional right reserved.

The information in the following pages is broadly considered a truthful and accurate account of facts and as such, any inattention, use, or misuse of the information in question by the reader will render any resulting actions solely under their purview. There are no scenarios in which the publisher or the original author of this work can be in any fashion deemed liable for any hardship or damages that may befall them after undertaking information described herein.

Additionally, the information in the following pages is intended only for informational purposes and should thus be thought of as universal. As befitting its nature, it is presented without assurance regarding its prolonged validity or interim quality. Trademarks that are mentioned are done without written consent and can in no way be considered an endorsement from the trademark holder.

Table of contents

The Right Mindset	7
Difficulties You Will Encounter and How to Solve Them	11
Keto-flu	12
Insomnia	14
Brain Fog	14
Constipation	15
Diarrhea	16
Keto Rash	17
Quick Recipes	19
Sweet Potato Hash	20
Celeriac Stuffed Avocado	22
Asparagus with Bacon and Eggs	24
Turkey Stuffed Peppers	26
Power Cream with Strawberry	28
Keto Chewy Chaffle	30
Keto Creamy Bacon Dish	32
Kale Mushroom Soup	34
Basil Stuffed Chicken	36
Haricots Verts Side Salad	38
Breakfast Recipes	41
Yogurt Waffles	42
Bacon Omelet	44
Green Shakshuka	46
Cheese Crepes	48
Lunch Recipes	51

Keto Sheet Pan Chicken and Rainbow Veggies	52
Skinny Bang-Bang Zucchini Noodles	54
Delicious Green Beans and Blue Cheese	56
Roasted Chicken	58
Boiled Garlic Clams	60
Rosemary-Lemon Shrimps	62
Salmon with Red Curry Sauce	64
Spicy Zoodles with Cheese	66
Steamed Herbed Red Snapper	68
Baked Salmon	70
Dinner Recipes	**73**
Chicken Casserole	74
Beef & Veggie Casserole	76
Beef with Bell Peppers	78
Braised Lamb Shanks	80
Beef Stir Fry	82
Sweet & Sour Pork	84
Mustard Pork Tenderloin	86
Dessert Recipes	**89**
Delicious Coffee Ice Cream	90
Fatty Bombs with Cinnamon and Cardamom	92
Easy Peanut Butter Cups	94
Chocolate Spread with Hazelnuts	96
Quick and Simple Brownie	98
Cute Peanut Balls	100
Condiment Recipes	**103**

Green Cilantro Sauce	104
Spicy Tahini Dressing	106
Appetizer and Snacks	109
Roasted Cauliflower	110
Spicy Pecans	112
Grilled Halloumi Cheese with Eggs	114
About the author	118

The Right Mindset

I'm not a motivator. But if you don't apply the right mental mindset, I'm sorry to tell you, but you'll never get results. Find your own reason; you have to be really incentivized to give a turning point to your life. You have to stay focused, especially at the beginning, because it will be difficult at the beginning when you are coming out of your comfort zone, so you are engaging, and this requires great motivation and also willpower.

It's likely that after you read this book, you'll put it in the library and forget the concepts. Instead, you have to be active already from now and do not allow bad thoughts to show up, change perspective if you have bad thoughts and focused on your goal and reach it, do not stop even one step from the finish line, and try to always keep a mindset oriented towards success, do not get knocked down by anything and anyone and if someone will try to hinder you means that what you are doing is the right way. The first change starts from your head; if you think you won't succeed, you have already failed at the start; for example, I hang writing on the walls of my room, and every day I observe them and sometimes read them out loud, this I need not shift the focus from my goals and always stay focused and find strength and mental energy when I want and when I need them, give yourself courage because there is nothing difficult if you really believe it.

Start changing your lifestyle and set yourself new goals,

and don't run away between diets; running away doesn't make it, so you're busy bringing the results home. Now make the best decision for yourself to make the ketogenic diet your new lifestyle. Then you'll be self-figuring out if it's for you or not, but I think as soon as you discover the great results that it will bring you in your life, I'm sure it will become your new best friend.

If you have a great preference for fatty foods, it is better for you. Now you have a choice ahead of you: give the keto diet a chance or give up and return to life as usual. If you choose the first path, consider the long term because it is very easy that when you reach your goals, once you reach them, you maybe will be inclined to abandon the diet, remember the sacrifices you have made and perceive how strong you feel thanks to it, then you will decide what is best for you if you need to look for answers look at the testimonies of people who thanks to the diet to have lost many kilos and are inspired by its results. If other people can do it, you can do it too, don't think that the keto diet doesn't work for you because it would be having a losing mentality and not looking towards results as it really should be. My advice is to really try and believe it; if you don't, your mental programming is continuing to give you self-justifications so as not to try, so reprogram your thoughts and use your mind as the best atonement. If there are any obstacles to force, do not allow them to stop, do not give them too much importance.

Dana Roberts

Difficulties You Will Encounter and How to Solve Them

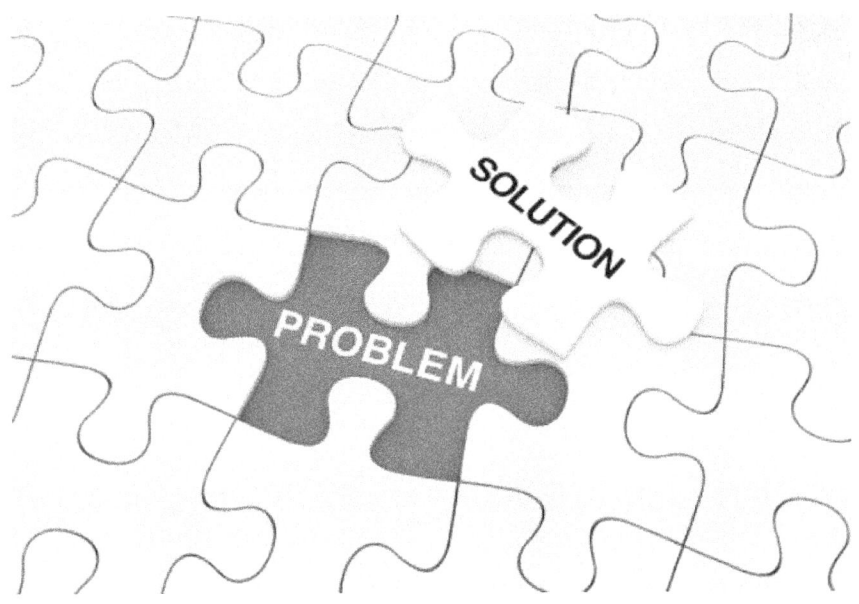

Keto diet is quite simple; just eat 75% fats, 20% protein, and 5% carbs. It is a general practice most ketogenic beginners follow, and they maintain their body quite quickly. However, when you cross the age of 50, there are many challenges which you have to go through. Below is the list of those challenges, along with their solutions.

Keto-flu

An abrupt shift of diet, from the normal intake of carbs to a limited amount, can cause keto-flu, also known as carb withdrawal. It usually occurs after one to two days of withdrawal. Its symptoms include headache, muscle soreness, poor focus, sugar cravings, brain fog, irritability, insomnia, or weakness. Your body will take some time to switch from burning carbohydrates to burning fats. Therefore, an abrupt transformation of diet sends your body into starvation mode, hence giving you those unpleasant symptoms. Follow the tips below to help you ease discomforts and symptoms of keto flu.

Stay well Hydrated

How much you should drink depends on your body weight. Divide your body weight by 2. The resulting number of ounces is the water you need to drink per day. The best way to add water is by consuming bone broth in your diet. It will provide not only electrolytes such as potassium and sodium to your body but also water.

Electrolytes Supplementation

Electrolytes such as sodium, magnesium, and potassium are the key players when it comes to getting better and faster results on a keto diet. If that is not enough in your body, which is usually common if you are on a low carb diet, try incorporating them by taking electrolytes supplements.

Consume More Healthy Fats

To enhance your adaptation phase, try to eat a lot of high-quality fat such as MCT oils because it travels straight to the liver after digestion as compared to other fats; hence it can be used immediately.

Consume exogenous Ketone Supplement

Exogenous ketone supplements aid fatigue and elevate energy levels by increasing the ketone levels in the blood. If you opt for this path, go for a smaller dose of these supplements. Take them, especially during the first five days of the keto flu.

Muscle cramps and Dehydration

Carbs need water for their storage, unlike fats. Hence, instead of being retained, a smaller amount of water is stored during the keto diet, and a substantial amount of sodium is excreted by the kidneys. Due to this, you can easily get dehydrated while on the keto diet, especially at the beginning. Due to this condition, low electrolyte concentration and dehydration, muscle cramping is certain.

Solution

- Consult your doctor and complain to him/her about the problems you are facing.

- Add electrolytes supplements, as discussed under keto flu, especially the three major electrolytes such as potassium, sodium, and magnesium.
- Ensure drinking a lot of water in order to remain hydrated; remember the rule of dividing your body weight by 2.

Insomnia

Although there is not any research that has shown the effect of a keto diet on sleep deprivation, there are some people who have complained about lack of quality sleep during the keto diet. If this is the case with you, then once in a while, eating some high-quality carbs before bed can prove to be of huge help.

Solution

Before sleeping, take one teaspoon of raw honey. This will give your body adequate high-quality carbs during your sleep.

Brain Fog

When you eat fewer carbs, your body demands it; "I am hungry, and I want something to eat." When its wish isn't accommodated, it makes you fuzzy-headed. This is the brain's way of demanding more glucose. Because, up until now, that's the only fuel it has ever known.

Solution

The best solution to remedy this condition is to ignore it and keep eating fat simply! Ultimately, your brain will adapt to its new fuel, and your head will become clearer than ever before.

Constipation

Consuming carbs lesser than 20g of per day means insufficient fibers, which ultimately results in constipation and irritable bowel syndrome. Constipation also occurs when you are not drinking enough water. The following are some remedies to aid you in your constipation.

Solution

- Add leafy and good vegetables to your diet.
- Try cyclical keto from time to time. This will enable you to eat foods like butternut squash and sweet potatoes.
- Add enough natural salt such as Himalayan pink salt in your diet to help you retain water and make your bowels regular.
- Always remain hydrated and take electrolytes supplements.
- Do exercise regularly; it will also help you in relieving constipation problems.

- Try to take the recommended dosage of a good-quality digestive enzyme before or after every meal.
- Consume psyllium husk every morning. Mix one teaspoon in ½ cup of water and let it sit for 1 minute before drinking.

Diarrhea

Some people have diarrhea difficulties while on the keto diet. Your body may react this way because of an increasing amount of fat intake, as it isn't yet able to produce and store enough bile to break down all the fat you're eating.

Solution

- Reduce the amount of fat you're eating by at least 10 percent.
- Simultaneously, increase the number of fermented foods in your diets such as kombucha, water kefir, sauerkraut, kimchi, or your favorite fermented vegetable.
- Add apple cider vinegar to your drinks and salad dressings.
- Consider trying an ox bile supplement.
- To cure diarrhea, lower your fat intake for seven days—or until you are adapted to the new changes. Then, gradually increase your fat intake back up to where it was.

Keto Rash

Keto rash, also called prurigo pigmentosa is an itchy red rash that can develop on the neck, chest, back, and armpit areas; it is neither dangerous nor life-threatening. Although very rare, it sometimes occurs when people follow a strict ketogenic diet, usually 80 percent fat or higher. Other causative agents are hormonal imbalances, allergens exposure, and gut bacteria.

Solution

- Support your skin with adequate supplements and anti-inflammatory foods such as DHA, omega-3 supplements, or turmeric latte. This will boost the healing time while soothing the rash.

- Keep yourself away from irritants like heat, sweat, or friction. The Keto rash, just like other rashes, can become worse when connecting with irritants. Avoid these irritants by putting on loose and breathable clothes, avoiding scented products or perfumes, or any sweat-stimulating exercise until your skin is properly healed.

- Reintroduce some carbs in your diet, though avoid consuming a lot of bread. However, if rash occurs after a sudden shift to a keto lifestyle, it is essential for you to bring back some high quality and healthy carbs such as butternut squash, pumpkin, carrots, yams, and sweet potatoes.

Quick Recipes

Sweet Potato Hash

Preparation time: 10 Minutes

Cooking time: 10 Minutes

Servings: 4

Ingredients:

- 1 Tablespoon Italian seasoning
- 6 Eggs
- 1 Sweet potato, cubed
- ½ Pound pork sausage, ground
- 1 Yellow onion, chopped

For the instant pot:

- 2 Cups water

Directions:

1. Set your instant pot on sauté mode, add onion, sausage, meat, and sweet potato, stir, cook for 5 minutes and transfer to a baking dish.
2. In a bowl, mix eggs with Italian seasoning, whisk well, and pour over the sausage mixture.
3. Add the water to your instant pot, add trivet, add baking dish inside, cover and cook on high for 5 minutes.
4. Leave hash to cool down a bit, divide between plates and serve.
5. Enjoy!

Nutrition:

- Calories: 216
- Fat: 6
- Fiber: 3
- Carbs: 12
- Protein: 5

Celeriac Stuffed Avocado

Preparation time: 5 minutes

Cooking time: 0 minutes

Servings: 2

Ingredients:

- ¼ Tsp. salt
- ½ of a lemon, juiced, zested
- 1 Avocado
- 1 Celery root, finely chopped
- 2 Tbsp mayonnaise

Directions:

1. Prepare avocado and for this, cut avocado in half and then remove its pit.
2. Put remaining ingredients in a bowl, mix until combined thoroughly, and evenly stuff this mixture into avocado halves.

Nutrition:

- Calories: 285
- Fats: 3g
- Carbohydrates: 3g
- Protein: 4g

Asparagus with Bacon and Eggs

Preparation time: 5 Minutes

Cooking time: 8 Minutes

Servings: 2

Ingredients:

- ¼ Tsp. salt
- 1 Egg

- 1/8 Tsp. ground black pepper
- 2 Slices of bacon, diced
- 4oz. Asparagus

Directions:

1. Bring out a skillet pan, put it over medium heat, add bacon, and cook for 4 min until crispy.
2. Move cooked bacon to a plate, then add asparagus into the pan and cook for 5 min until tender-crisp.
3. Crack the egg over the cooked asparagus, season with salt and black pepper, then switch heat to medium-low level and cook for 2 min until the egg white has set.
4. Chop the cooked bacon slices, sprinkle over egg and asparagus and serve.

Nutrition:

- Calories: 179 Fats: 153g
- Carbohydrates: 1g
- Protein: 2g

Turkey Stuffed Peppers

Servings: 4

Ingredients:

- 2 Large sweet peppers, halved and seeded
- 1 Teaspoon garlic salt
- 12oz. Ground turkey
- 3/4 Cup ricotta cheese
- 1 Cup mozzarella

Directions:

1. Preheat the oven to 400 degrees F.
2. Place the pepper halves in a baking dish and drizzle ¼ teaspoons garlic salt on the top.
3. Divide the ground turkey into each pepper half.
4. Drizzle remaining garlic salt on top.
5. Bake the peppers for 25 minutes in the preheated oven.
6. Top the stuffed peppers with ricotta cheese and mozzarella cheese.
7. Bake the peppers again for 5 minutes to melt the cheese.
8. Serve warm.

Nutrition:

- Calories 267 Total Fat 14.4g
- Saturated Fat 4.7g Cholesterol 105mg
- Sodium 194mg Total Carbohydrate 6.4g
- Dietary Fiber 1.4g Total Sugars 2.1g
- Protein 31.3g

Power Cream with Strawberry

Preparation time: 5 Minutes

Cooking time: 0

Servings: 2

Ingredients:

- 1 Tbsp coconut oil
- 2 Tsp. vanilla extract, unsweetened
- 4oz. Coconut cream, full-fat

- 4oz. Fresh strawberries

Directions:

1. Bring out a large bowl, put all the ingredients in it, and then mix by using a blender until smooth.
2. Distribute evenly between two bowls and then serve.

Nutrition:

- Calories: 214
- Fats: 3g
- Carbohydrates: 2g
- Protein: 4g

Keto Chewy Chaffle

Preparation time: 5 Minutes

Cooking time: 5 Minutes

Servings: 2

Ingredients:

- ½ Cup shredded mozzarella cheese, full-fat
- 1 Egg, pasteurized
- 2 Tsp. coconut flour

Directions:

1. Turn on a mini waffle maker and let it preheat for 5 minutes.
2. In the meantime, bring out a medium bowl, put all the ingredients in it, and then mix by using a blender until smooth.
3. Scoop the batter evenly into the waffle maker, shut with lid, and let it cook for 3 to 4 minutes until firm and golden brown.

Nutrition:

- Calories: 142
- Fats: 10g
- Carbohydrates: 1g
- Protein: 3g

Keto Creamy Bacon Dish

Preparation time: 5 minutes

Cooking time: 7 minutes

Servings: 2

Ingredients:

- ½ Tsp. dried basil
- ½ Tsp. minced garlic
- ½ Tsp. tomato paste

- 2oz unsalted butter, softened
- 3 Slices of bacon, chopped

Directions:

1. Bring out a skillet pan, put it over medium heat, add 1 tbsp butter and when it starts to melts, add chopped bacon and cook for 5 minutes.
2. Then remove the pan from heat, add remaining butter, along with basil and tomato paste, season with salt and black pepper, and stir.
3. Move bacon butter into an airtight container, cover with the lid, and refrigerate for 1 hour until solid.

Nutrition:

- Calories: 150
- Fats: 16g
- Carbohydrates: 1g
- Protein: 1g

Kale Mushroom Soup

Preparation time: 16 Minutes.

Cooking time: 60 Minutes.

Servings: 4

Ingredients:

- 1lb. Sausage cooked, casings removed and sliced
- 29oz. Chicken bone broth
- 6 ½ oz. Fresh kale, cut into bite-sized pieces
- 6 ½ oz. Sliced mushrooms

- 2 Garlic cloves, minced
- Salt and black pepper to taste

Directions:

1. Pour chicken broth and an equal amount of water into a cooking pot.
2. Place the pot on medium heat and cook to a boil.
3. Stir in mushrooms, garlic, sausage, and kale.
4. Adjust seasoning with black pepper and salt.
5. Cover and cook the broccoli soup on low heat for 1 hour. Serve warm.

Nutrition:

- Calories: 276 Total Fat: 20g
- Saturated Fat: 6g Cholesterol: 54mg
- Sodium: 995mg Total Carbohydrate: 4g
- Dietary Fiber: 0.2g Total Sugars: 0g
- Protein: 14g

Basil Stuffed Chicken

Preparation time: 14 Minutes.

Cooking time: 45 Minutes.

Servings: 4

Ingredients:

- 2 Chicken breasts, bone-in, skin-on
- 2 Tablespoons cream cheese
- 2 Tablespoons mozzarella cheese, shredded
- ¼ Teaspoons garlic paste

- 3 Fresh basil leaves, chopped
- Black pepper, to taste

Directions:

1. Preheat your oven to 375 degrees F.
2. Mix cream cheese with garlic paste, shredded cheese, black pepper, and basil in a bowl. Gently cut each of the chicken breast's skin from one side and stuff the cream cheese mixture inside.
3. Place the prepared chicken on the baking sheet and bake them for 45 minutes in the preheated oven. Serve warm.

Nutrition:

- Calories: 362 Total Fat: 7.3g
- Saturated Fat: 3.2g Cholesterol: 204mg
- Sodium: 937mg Total Carbohydrate: 0.3g
- Dietary Fiber: 0g
- Total Sugars: 0g Protein: 76.2g

Haricots Verts Side Salad

Preparation time: 10 Minutes

Cooking time: 8 Minutes

Servings: 4

Ingredients:

- 4 Ounces pancetta, chopped
- 2 Pounds haricots verts
- ½ Cup dates, sliced
- ½ Cup chicken stock
- Black pepper to the taste

Directions:

1. Set your instant pot on sauté mode, add pancetta, stir and cook for 3 minutes.

2. Add haricot verts, dates, and black pepper, stir and cook for 2 minutes more.
3. Add stock, stir a bit more, cover and cook on high for 3 minutes.
4. Divide everything between plates and serve as a side dish.
5. Enjoy!

Nutrition:

- Calories: 128 Fat: 3
- Fiber: 6 Carbs: 16 Protein: 4

Dana Roberts

Breakfast Recipes

Yogurt Waffles

Preparation time: 15 Minutes

Cooking time: 25 Minutes

Servings: 4

Ingredients:

- ½ Cup golden flax seeds meal
- ½ Cup plus 3 tablespoons almond flour
- 1-1½ Tablespoons granulated erythritol
- 1 Tablespoon unsweetened vanilla whey protein powder
- ½ Teaspoon organic powder
- ¼ Teaspoon xanthan gum
- Salt, as required
- 1 Large organic egg, white and yolk separated
- 1 Organic whole egg
- 2 Tablespoons unsweetened almond milk

- 1½ Tablespoons unsalted butter
- 3 Ounces plain Greek yogurt
- ¼ Teaspoon baking soda

Directions:

1. Preheat the waffle iron and then grease it.
2. In a large bowl, add the flour, erythritol, protein powder, baking soda, baking powder, xanthan gum, and salt, and mix until well combined.
3. In a second small bowl, add the egg white and beat until stiff peaks form.
4. In a third bowl, add two egg yolks, whole egg, almond milk, butter, and yogurt, and beat until well combined.
5. Place egg mixture into the bowl of the flour mixture and mix until well combined.
6. Gently fold in the beaten egg whites.
7. Place ¼ cup of the mixture into preheated waffle iron and cook for about 4–5 minutes or until golden brown.
8. Repeat with the remaining mixture.
9. Serve warm.

Nutrition:

- Calories: 250 Net Carbs: 3.2g
- Total Carbs: 8.8g Fiber: 5.6g
- Sugar: 1.3g Protein: 8.4g

Bacon Omelet

Preparation time: 10 Minutes

Cooking time: 15 Minutes

Servings: 3

Ingredients:

- 4 Large organic eggs
- 1 Tablespoon fresh chives, minced
- Salt and ground black pepper, as required
- 4 Bacon slices
- 1 Tablespoon unsalted butter
- 2 Ounces cheddar cheese, shredded

Directions:

1. In a bowl, add the eggs, chives, salt, and black pepper, and beat until well combined.

2. Heat a non-stick frying pan over medium-high heat and cook the bacon slices for about 8–10 minutes.
3. Place the bacon onto a paper towel-lined plate to drain. Then chop the bacon slices.
4. With paper towels, wipe out the frying pan.
5. In the same frying pan, melt butter over medium-low heat and cook the egg mixture for about 2 minutes.
6. Carefully flip the omelet and top with chopped bacon.
7. Cook for 1–2 minutes or until the desired doneness of eggs.
8. Remove from heat and immediately place the cheese in the center of the omelet.
9. Fold the omelet edges over the cheese and cut into two portions.
10. Serve immediately.

Nutrition:

- Calories: 427 Net Carbs: 1.2g
- Total Carbs: 1.2g Fiber: 0g
- Sugar: 1g Protein: 29.1g

Green Shakshuka

Preparation time: 15 Minutes

Cooking time: 10 Minutes

Servings: 4

Ingredients:

- 1 Tbsp. olive oil
- 2 Tbsp. almond oil
- 1/2 Medium green bell pepper, deseeded and chopped
- 1 Celery stalk, chopped
- 1/4 Cup (57 g) green beans, chopped
- 1 Garlic clove, minced
- 2 Tbsp. fresh mint leaves

- 3 Tbsp. fresh parsley leaves
- 1/2 Cup (113 g) baby kale
- 1/4 Tsp. plain vinegar
- Salt and black pepper to taste
- 1/4 Tsp. nutmeg powder
- 7oz. (200 g) feta cheese, divided
- 4 Eggs

Directions:

1. Heat the olive oil and almond oil in a medium frying pan over medium heat.
2. Add the bell pepper, celery, green beans, and sauté for 5 minutes or until the vegetables soften.
3. Stir in the garlic, mint leaves, two tablespoons of parsley, and cook until fragrant, 1 minute.
4. Add the kale, vinegar, and mix. Once the kale starts wilting, season with salt, black pepper, nutmeg powder, and stir in half of the feta cheese—Cook for 1 to 2 minutes.
5. After, use the spatula to create four holes in the food and crack an egg into each hole. Cook until the egg whites set still running.
6. Season the eggs with salt and black pepper.
7. Turn the heat off and scatter the remaining feta cheese on top.
8. Garnish with the remaining parsley and serve the shakshuka immediately.

Nutrition:

- Calories: 322
- Fat: 14.1g
- Fiber: 10.3g
- Carbohydrates: 9.4g

Cheese Crepes

Preparation time: 15 Minutes

Cooking time: 20 Minutes

Servings: 4

Ingredients:

- 6 Ounces cream cheese, softened
- 1/3 Cup Parmesan cheese, grated
- 6 Large organic eggs
- 1 Teaspoon granulated erythritol
- 1½ Tablespoon coconut flour
- 1/8 Teaspoon xanthan gum

- 2 Tablespoons unsalted butter

Directions:

1. In a blender, add cream cheese, Parmesan cheese, eggs, and erythritol, and pulse on low speed until well mixed.
2. While the motor is running, place the coconut flour and xanthan gum and pulse until a thick mixture is formed.
3. Now, pulse on medium speed for a few seconds.
4. Transfer the mixture into a bowl and set aside for about 5 minutes.
5. Divide the mixture into ten equal-sized portions.
6. In a nonstick pan, melt butter over medium-low heat.
7. Place one portion of the mixture and tilt the pan to spread into a thin layer.
8. Cook for about 1½ minutes or until the edges become brown.
9. Flip the crepe and cook for about 15-20 seconds more.
10. Repeat with the remaining mixture.
11. Serve warm with your favorite keto-friendly filling.

Nutrition:

- Calories: 297
- Net Carbs: 1.9g
- Total Carbs: 3.5g
- Fiber: 1.6g
- Sugar: 0.5g
- Protein: 13.7g
-

Dana Roberts

Lunch Recipes

Keto Sheet Pan Chicken and Rainbow Veggies

Preparation time: 15 Minutes

Cooking time: 25 Minutes

Servings: 4

Ingredients:

- Nonstick spray
- 1 Pound Chicken Breasts

- 1 Tbsp. Sesame Oil
- 2 Tbsp. Soy Sauce
- 2 Tbsp. Honey
- 2 Red Pepper
- 2 Yellow Pepper
- 3 Carrots
- ½ Broccoli
- 2 Red Onions
- 2 Tbsp. EVOO
- Pepper & salt
- .25 c Parsley

Directions:

1. Grease the baking sheet, warm-up the oven to a temperature of 400-degrees.
2. Put the chicken in the middle of the sheet. Separately, combine the oil and the soy sauce. Brush over the chicken.
3. Separate veggies across the plate. Sprinkle with oil and then toss. Put pepper & salt.
4. Set tray into the oven and cook within 25 minutes. Garnish using parsley. Serve.

Nutrition:

- Net Carbs: 9g Fiber: 0g
- Fat: 30g Protein: 30g Calories: 437kcal

Skinny Bang-Bang Zucchini Noodles

Preparation time: 15 Minutes

Cooking time: 15 Minutes

Servings: 4

Ingredients:

For the noodles:

- 4 Medium zucchinis spiraled
- 1 Tbsp. olive oil

For the sauce:

- 0.25 Cup + 2 tablespoons Plain Greek Yogurt
- 0.25 Cup + 2 tablespoons Mayo
- 0.25 Cup + 2 tablespoons Thai Sweet Chili Sauce
- 1.5 Teaspoons Honey
- 1.5 Teaspoons Sriracha
- 2 Teaspoons Lime Juice

Directions:

1. Pour the oil into a large skillet at medium temperature. Stir in the spiraled zucchini noodles.
2. Remove then drain, and let it rest 10 minutes. Combine sauce items into a bowl.
3. Mix in the noodles to the sauce. Serve.

Nutrition:

- Net Carbs: 18g Fiber: 0g
- Fat: 1g Protein: 9g Calories: 161g
- Protein: 13.1g

Delicious Green Beans and Blue Cheese

Preparation time: 10 Minutes

Cooking time: 7 Minutes

Servings: 4

Ingredients:

- 1 and ½ Pounds green beans
- ½ Cup almonds, chopped
- ¼ Cup olive oil
- 2 Tablespoons blue cheese, crumbled
- 2 Tablespoons lemon juice

For the instant pot:

- ½ Cup water

Directions:

1. Put the water in your instant pot, add steamer basket, add green beans inside, cover, cook on high for 2 minutes, drain and transfer them to a bowl.
2. Clean the pot, set on sauté mode, add oil, heat it up, add green beans, stir and cook for 3 minutes.
3. Add lemon juice and almonds, stir and cook for 2 minutes more.
4. Divide on plates, sprinkle blue cheese all over, and serve as a side dish. Enjoy!

Nutrition:

- Calories: 200 Fat: 4
- Fiber: 4 Carbs: 7 Protein: 4

Roasted Chicken

Preparation time: 18 Minutes

Cooking time: 30 Minutes

Servings: 6

Ingredients:

- 2lbs. Chicken breast, cooked and diced
- 1 1/2 Cups vodka sauce jarred
- 1/2 Cup parmesan cheese
- 16oz. Fresh mozzarella

Directions:

1. Preheat the oven to 400 degrees F.
2. Grease a casserole dish with cooking spray.
3. Spread the cooked chicken in the casserole dish.
4. Add vodka sauce, mozzarella, and parmesan cheese on top.
5. Bake the saucy chicken casserole for 30 minutes in the preheated oven.
6. Serve warm.

Nutrition:

- Calories: 446 Fat: 23g
- Carbohydrate: 3g Protein: 52g

Boiled Garlic Clams

Preparation time: 3 Minutes

Cooking time: 10 Minutes

Servings: 6

Ingredients:

- 3 Tbsp butter
- 6 Cloves of garlic
- 50 Small clams in the shell, scrubbed
- ½ Cup fresh parsley, chopped
- 4 Tbsp. extra virgin olive oil

Directions:

1. In a large pot placed on medium-high fire, heat the butter and olive oil for a minute.
2. Stir in the garlic and cook until fragrant and slightly browned.
3. Stir in the clams, water, and parsley—season with salt and pepper to taste.
4. Cover and cook for 5 minutes or until clams have opened.
5. Discard unopened clams and serve.

Nutrition:

- Calories: 159
- Fat: 12.8g
- Carbohydrates: 0.9g
- Protein: 11.3g

Rosemary-Lemon Shrimps

Preparation time: 3 Minutes

Cooking time: 8 Minutes

Servings: 8

Ingredients:

- 5 Tablespoons butter
- ½ Cup lemon juice, freshly squeezed
- 1 ½ lb. Shrimps, peeled and deveined
- ¼ Cup coconut aminos
- 1 Tsp. rosemary

Directions:

1. Put all ingredients in a large pan on a high fire.
2. Boil for 8 minutes or until shrimps are pink.
3. Serve and enjoy.

Nutrition:

- Calories: 315 Fat: 17.9g
- Carbohydrates: 3.7g Protein: 35.8g

Salmon with Red Curry Sauce

Preparation time: 10 Minutes

Cooking time: 22 Minutes

Servings: 4

Ingredients: 4 Salmon fillets

- 2 Tablespoons olive oil
- Salt and pepper to taste
- 1 ½ Tablespoons red curry paste
- 1 Tablespoon fresh ginger, chopped
- 14oz. Coconut cream
- 1 ½ Tablespoons fish sauce

Directions:

1. Preheat your oven to 350 degrees F.
2. Cover baking sheet with foil.
3. Brush both sides of salmon fillets with olive oil and season with salt and pepper.
4. Place the salmon fillets on the baking sheet. Bake salmon in the oven for 20 minutes.
5. In a pan over medium heat, mix the curry paste, ginger, coconut cream, and fish sauce. Sprinkle with salt and pepper.
6. Simmer for 2 minutes. Pour the sauce over the salmon before serving.

Nutrition:

- Calories: 553 Total Fat: 43.4g
- Saturated Fat: 24.1g Cholesterol: 78mg
- Sodium: 908mg Total Carbohydrate: 7.9g
- Dietary Fiber: 2.4g Total Sugars: 3.6g
- Protein: 37.3g Potassium: 982mg

Spicy Zoodles with Cheese

Preparation time: 10 Minutes

Cooking time: 6 Minutes

Servings: 2

Ingredients:

- 1 ½ Tsp. minced garlic
- 1 Large zucchini, spiralized into noodles
- 2 Tbsp. grated parmesan cheese
- 2 Tbsp. unsalted butter

Directions:

1. Prepare zucchini noodles, and for this, cut zucchini into noodles by using a spiralizer or a vegetable peeler, and then set aside until required.
2. Bring out a skillet pan, place it over medium-high heat, add butter and garlic, cook for 1 minute until garlic is fragrant, then add zucchini noodles and continue cooking for 3 to 5 minutes until al dente.
3. When done, remove the skillet pan from heat, season zucchini noodles with salt, red chili flakes, and black pepper, add cheese, and stir well until mixed.

Nutrition:

- Calories: 150 Fats: 16g
- Protein: 1g Net Carbs: 0.5g Fiber: 1g

Steamed Herbed Red Snapper

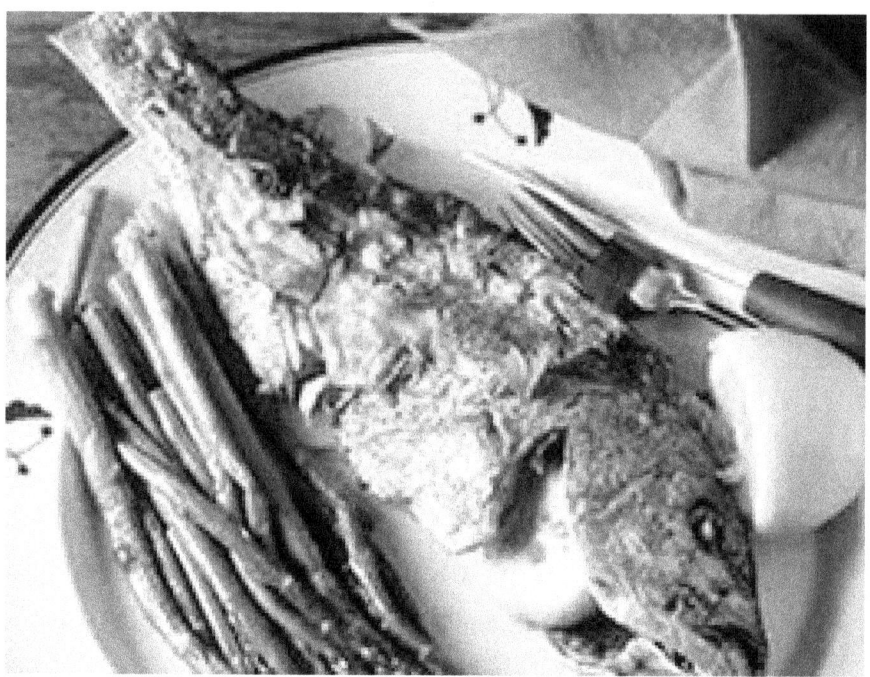

Preparation time: 3 Minutes

Cooking time: 15 Minutes

Servings: 4

Ingredients:

- 4 Red snapper fillets
- ¼ Tsp. paprika
- 3 Tbsp. lemon juice, freshly squeezed
- 1 ½ Tsp. chopped fresh herbs of your choice (rosemary, thyme, basil, or parsley)

Directions:

1. In a small bowl, whisk well paprika, lemon juice, olive oil, and herbs. Season with pepper and salt.
2. Place a trivet in a large saucepan and pour a cup or two of water into the pan. Bring to a boil.
3. Place snapper in a heatproof dish that fits inside a saucepan—season snapper with pepper and salt. Drizzle with lemon mixture.
4. Seal dish with foil. Place the dish on the trivet inside the saucepan—cover and steam for 15 minutes.
5. Serve and enjoy.

Nutrition:

- Calories: 374 Fat: 20.3g
- Carbohydrates: 2.1g Protein: 45.6g

Baked Salmon

Preparation time: 10 Minutes

Cooking time: 10 Minutes

Servings: 4

Ingredients:

- Cooking spray
- 3 Cloves garlic, minced
- ¼ Cup butter
- 1 Teaspoon lemon zest
- 2 Tablespoons lemon juice
- 4 Salmon fillets
- Salt and pepper to taste
- 2 Tablespoons parsley, chopped

Directions:

1. Preheat your oven to 425 degrees F.
2. Grease the pan with cooking spray.
3. In a bowl, mix the garlic, butter, lemon zest, and lemon juice.
4. Sprinkle salt and pepper on salmon fillets.
5. Drizzle with the lemon butter sauce.
6. Bake in the oven for 12 minutes.
7. Garnish with parsley before serving.

Nutrition:

- Calories: 345 Total Fat: 22.7g
- Saturated Fat: 8.9g Cholesterol: 109mg
- Sodium: 163mg Total Carbohydrate: 1.2g
- Dietary Fiber: 0.2g Total Sugars: 0.2g
- Protein: 34.9g Potassium: 718mg

Dana Roberts

Dinner Recipes

Chicken Casserole

Preparation time: 15 Minutes

Cooking time: 1 Hour 10 minutes

Servings: 6

Ingredients:

Chicken Layer:

- 6 Grass-fed chicken breasts
- Salt
- Ground black pepper

Bacon Layer:

- 5 Bacon slices
- ¼ Cup yellow onion
- ¼ Cup jalapeño pepper
- ½ Cup mayonnaise

- 1 Package cream cheese
- ½ Cup Parmesan cheese
- 1 Cup cheddar cheese

Topping:

- 1 Package pork skins
- ¼ Cup butter
- ½ Cup Parmesan cheese

Directions:

1. Warm-up oven to 4250F.
2. Put the chicken breasts in the greased casserole, then put salt and black pepper.
3. Bake within 30–40 minutes.

For the bacon layer:

1. Cook the bacon within 8–10 minutes and transfer.
2. Sauté onion within 4–5 minutes. Remove, stir in bacon, and remaining fixing.
3. Remove the casserole dish, then put the bacon mixture.
4. Mix all topping fixing. Place the topping over the bacon mixture.
5. Bake within 15 minutes. Serve.

Nutrition:

- Calories: 826
- Net Carbs: 2.5g
- Total Fat: 62.9g
- Protein: 60.6g

Beef & Veggie Casserole

Preparation time: 20 Minutes

Cooking time: 55 Minutes

Servings: 6

Ingredients:

- 3 Tbsp. butter
- 1 Pound grass-fed ground beef
- 1 Yellow onion
- 2 Garlic cloves
- 1 Cup pumpkin
- 1 Cup broccoli

- 2 Cups cheddar cheese
- 1 Tbsp. Dijon mustard
- 6 Organic eggs
- ½ Cup heavy whipping cream
- Salt
- Ground black pepper

Directions:

1. Cook the beef within 8–10 minutes and transfer.
2. Cook the onion and garlic within 10 minutes. Add the pumpkin and cook within 5–6 minutes.
3. Add the broccoli and cook within 3–4 minutes. Transfer to the cooked beef, combine.
4. Warm-up oven to 350ºF.
5. Put 2/3 of cheese and mustard in the beef mixture, combine.
6. In another mixing bowl, add cream, eggs, salt, and black pepper, and beat.
7. Place the beef mixture and top with the egg mixture in a baking dish, plus the remaining cheese.
8. Bake within 25 minutes. Serve.

Nutrition: Calories 472 Net Carbs 5.5g

- Total Fat 34.6g Sodium 463mg
- Protein 32.6g

Beef with Bell Peppers

Preparation time: 15 Minutes

Cooking time: 10 Minutes

Servings: 4

Ingredients:

- 1 Tbsp. olive oil
- 1 Pound grass-fed flank steak
- 1 Red bell pepper
- 1 Green bell pepper

- 1 Tbsp. ginger
- 3 Tbsp. low-sodium soy sauce
- 1½ Tbsp. balsamic vinegar
- 2 Tsp. Sriracha

Directions:

1. Sear the steak slices within 2 minutes. Cook bell peppers within 2–3 minutes.
2. Transfer the beef mixture.
3. Boil the remaining fixing within 1 minute.
4. Add the beef mixture and cook within 1–2 minutes. Serve.

Nutrition:

- Calories: 274
- Net Carbs: 3.8g
- Total Fat: 13.1g
- Protein: 32.9g

Braised Lamb Shanks

Preparation time: 15 Minutes

Cooking time: 2 Hours 35 minutes

Servings: 4

Ingredients:

- 4 Grass-fed lamb shanks
- 2 Tbsp. butter
- Salt
- Ground black pepper
- 6 Garlic cloves
- 6 Rosemary sprigs
- 1 Cup chicken broth

Directions:

1. Warm-up oven to 450ºF.
2. Coat the shanks with butter and put salt plus pepper. Roast within 20 minutes.
3. Remove then reduce to 325ºF.
4. Place the garlic cloves and rosemary over and around the lamb.
5. Roast within 2 hours. Put the broth into a roasting pan.
6. Increase to 400ºF. Roast within 15 minutes more. Serve.

Nutrition:

- Calories: 1093 Net Carbs: 2g
- Total Fat: 44.2g Protein: 161.4g

Beef Stir Fry

Preparation time: 15 Minutes

Cooking time: 10 Minutes

Servings: 4

Ingredients:

- 1 Tablespoon soy sauce
- 1 Tablespoon ginger, minced
- 1 Teaspoon cornstarch
- 1 Teaspoon dry sherry
- 12oz. Beef, sliced into strips
- 1 Teaspoon toasted sesame oil
- 2 Tablespoons oyster sauce

- 1lb. Baby bok choy, sliced
- 3 Tablespoons chicken broth

Directions:

1. Mix soy sauce, ginger, cornstarch, and dry sherry in a bowl.
2. Toss the beef in the mixture.
3. Pour oil into a pan over medium heat.
4. Cook the beef for 5 minutes, stirring.
5. Add oyster sauce, bok choy, and chicken broth to the pan.
6. Cook for 1 minute.

Nutrition:

- Calories: 247 Total Fat: 15.8g
- Saturated Fat: 4g Cholesterol: 69mg
- Sodium: 569mg
- Total Carbohydrate: 6.3g
- Dietary Fiber 1.1g Protein: 25g

Sweet & Sour Pork

Preparation time: 15 Minutes

Cooking time: 15 Minutes

Servings: 4

Ingredients:

- 1lb. Pork chops
- Salt and pepper to taste
- ½ Cup sesame seeds

- 2 Tablespoons peanut oil
- 2 Tablespoons soy sauce
- 3 Tablespoons apricot jam
- Chopped scallions

Directions:

1. Season pork chops with salt and pepper.
2. Press sesame seeds on both sides of pork.
3. Pour oil into a pan over medium heat.
4. Cook pork for 3 to 5 minutes per side.
5. Transfer to a plate.
6. In a bowl, mix soy sauce and apricot jam.
7. Simmer for 3 minutes.
8. Pour sauce over the pork and garnish with scallions before serving.

Nutrition:

- Calories: 414 Total Fat: 27.5g
- Saturated Fat: 5.6g Cholesterol: 68mg
- Sodium: 607mg
- Total Carbohydrate: 12.9g
- Dietary Fiber: 1.8g Protein: 29g
- Total Sugars: 9g Potassium: 332mg

Mustard Pork Tenderloin

Preparation time: 15 Minutes

Cooking time: 30 Minutes

Servings: 3

Ingredients:

- 1 Tsp. fresh rosemary, minced
- 1 Garlic clove, minced
- 1 Tbsp. fresh lemon juice
- 1 Tbsp. olive oil
- 1 Tsp. Dijon mustard
- 1 Tsp. powdered Swerve
- Salt and freshly ground black pepper, to taste
- 1 lb. Pork tenderloin
- ¼ C. Blue cheese, crumbled

Directions:

1. Preheat oven to 4000 F. Grease a large rimmed baking sheet.
2. In a large bowl, add all the ingredients except the pork tenderloin and cheese and beat until well combined.
3. Add the pork tenderloin and coat with the mixture generously.
4. Arrange the pork tenderloin onto the prepared baking sheet.
5. Bake for about 20-22 minutes.
6. Remove from the oven and place the pork tenderloin onto a cutting board for about 5 minutes.
7. With a sharp knife, cut the pork tenderloin into ¾-inch thick slices and serve with cheese topping.

Nutrition:

- Calories per serving: 227
- Carbohydrates: 2g
- Protein: 37g
- Fat: 10g
- Sugar: 0.5g
- Sodium: 236mg
- Fiber: 0.1g

Dana Roberts

Dessert Recipes

Delicious Coffee Ice Cream

Preparation time: 10 Minutes

Cooking time: 5 Minutes

Servings: 1

Ingredients:

- 6 Ounces coconut cream, frozen into ice cubes
- 1 Ripe avocado, diced and frozen
- ½ Cup coffee expresso
- 2 Tbsp. sweetener
- 1 Tsp. vanilla extract
- 1 Tbsp. water
- Coffee beans

Directions:

- Take out the frozen coconut cubes and avocado from the fridge. Slightly melt them for 5-10 minutes.
- Add the sweetener, coffee expresso, and vanilla extract to the coconut-avocado mix and whisk with an immersion blender until it becomes creamy (for about 1 minute). Pour in the water and blend for 30 seconds.
- Top with coffee beans and enjoy!

Nutrition:

- Carbohydrates: 20.5g
- Fat: 61g
- Protein: 6.3g
- Calories: 596

Fatty Bombs with Cinnamon and Cardamom

Preparation time: 10 Minutes

Cooking time: 35 Minutes

Servings: 10

Ingredients:

- ½ Cup unsweetened coconut, shredded
- 3oz. Unsalted butter
- ¼ Tsp ground green cinnamon
- ¼ Ground cardamom
- ½ Tsp vanilla extract

Directions:

1. Roast the unsweetened coconut (choose medium-high heat) until it begins to turn lightly brown.
2. Combine the room-temperature butter, half of the shredded coconut, cinnamon, cardamom, and vanilla extract in a separate dish. Cool the mix in the fridge for about 5-10 minutes.
3. Form small balls and cover them with the remaining shredded coconut.
4. Cool the balls in the fridge for about 10-15 minutes.

Nutrition:

- Carbohydrates: 0.4g
- Fat: 10g
- Protein: 0.4g
- Calories: 90

Easy Peanut Butter Cups

Preparation time: 10 Minutes

Cooking time: 1 Hour 35 minutes

Servings: 12

Ingredients:

- 1/2 Cup peanut butter
- 1/4 Cup butter
- 3oz. Cacao butter, chopped
- 1/3 Cup powdered swerve sweetener
- 1/2 Tsp. vanilla extract
- 4oz. Sugar-free dark chocolate

Directions:

1. Line a muffin tin with parchment paper or cupcake liners.
2. Using low heat, melt the peanut butter, butter, and cacao butter in a saucepan. Stir them until completely combined.
3. Add the vanilla and sweetener until there are no more lumps.
4. Carefully place the mixture in the muffin cups.
5. Refrigerate it until firm
6. Put the chocolate in a bowl and set the bowl in boiling water. This is done to avoid direct contact with the heat. Stir the chocolate until completely melted.
7. Take the muffin out of the fridge and drizzle in the chocolate on top. Put it back again in the fridge to firm it up. This should take 15 minutes to finish.
8. Store and serve when needed.

Nutrition:
- Calories: 200k
- Fat: 19g
- Carbohydrates: 6g Protein: 2.9g
- Fiber: 3.6g

Chocolate Spread with Hazelnuts

Preparation time: 5 Minutes

Cooking time: 5 Minutes

Servings: 6

Ingredients:

- 2 Tbsp. cacao powder
- 5oz. Hazelnuts, roasted and without shells
- 1oz. Unsalted butter
- ¼ Cup coconut oil

Directions:

1. Whisk all the spread ingredients with a blender for as long as you want. Remember, the longer you blend, the smoother your spread.

Nutrition:

- Calories: 271 Carbohydrates: 2g
- Fat: 28g Protein: 4g

Quick and Simple Brownie

Preparation time: 20 Minutes

Cooking time: 5 Minutes

Servings: 2

Ingredients:

- 3 Tbsp. Keto chocolate chips
- 1 Tbsp. unsweetened cacao powder
- 2 Tbsp. salted butter
- 2¼ Tbsp. powdered sugar

Directions:

1. Combine two tablespoons of chocolate chips and butter, melt them in a microwave for 10-15 minutes. Add the remaining chocolate chips, stir and make a sauce.
2. Add the cacao powder and powdered sugar to the sauce and whisk well until you have a dough.
3. Place the dough on a baking sheet, form the Brownie.
4. Put your Brownie into the oven (preheated to 350°F).
5. Bake for 5 minutes.

Nutrition:

- Carbohydrates: 9g
- Fat: 30g
- Protein: 13g
- Calories: 100

Cute Peanut Balls

Preparation time: 20 Minutes

Cooking time: 20 Minutes

Servings: 18

Ingredients:

- 1 Cup salted peanuts, chopped
- 1 Cup peanut butter
- 1 Cup powdered sweetener
- 8oz keto chocolate chips

Directions:

1. Combine the chopped peanuts, peanut butter, and sweetener in a separate dish. Stir well and make a dough. Divide it into 18 pieces and form small balls. Put them in the fridge for 10-15 minutes.
2. Use a microwave to melt your chocolate chips.
3. Plunge each ball into the melted chocolate.
4. Return your balls to the fridge. Cool for about 20 minutes.

Nutrition:

- Calories: 194 Carbohydrates: 7g
- Fat: 17g Protein: 7g

Dana Roberts

Condiment Recipes

Green Cilantro Sauce

Preparation time: 5 Minutes

Cooking time: 20 Minutes

Servings: 10

Ingredients:

- 2 Cup olive oil
- 1 Cup cilantro
- 5 Tablespoons water
- 4 Garlic cloves

- ¼ Tablespoon ground cumin
- Sherry

Directions:

1. To begin this sauce, you will want to crush your garlic cloves and place them into a food processor along with the cilantro.
2. After you have processed these two ingredients together, slowly add in your olive oil and smoothly blend everything together.
3. If you would like, feel welcome to combine as much or as little water as you would like, along with the sherry vinegar for some extra flavor.
4. Finally, add in your ground cumin, stir, and the sauce will be prepared.

Nutrition:

- Calories: 80
- Carbs: 11g
- Fat: 3g
- Protein: 2g

Spicy Tahini Dressing

Preparation time: 5 Minutes

Cooking time: 0 Minutes

Servings: 3

Ingredients:

- ¼ Cup apple cider vinegar
- ½ Cup nutritional yeast
- ¼ Cup tahini
- ¼ Cup lemon juice
- 1 Tablespoon garlic
- ¼ Cup tamari sauce

Directions:

1. If you like your dressing with a little kick, give this recipe a try. Simply place all into a blender, blend on high for twenty seconds, and then enjoy.

Nutrition:

- Calories: 50
- Carbs: 1g
- Fat: 12g
- Protein: 2g

Dana Roberts

Appetizer and Snacks

Roasted Cauliflower

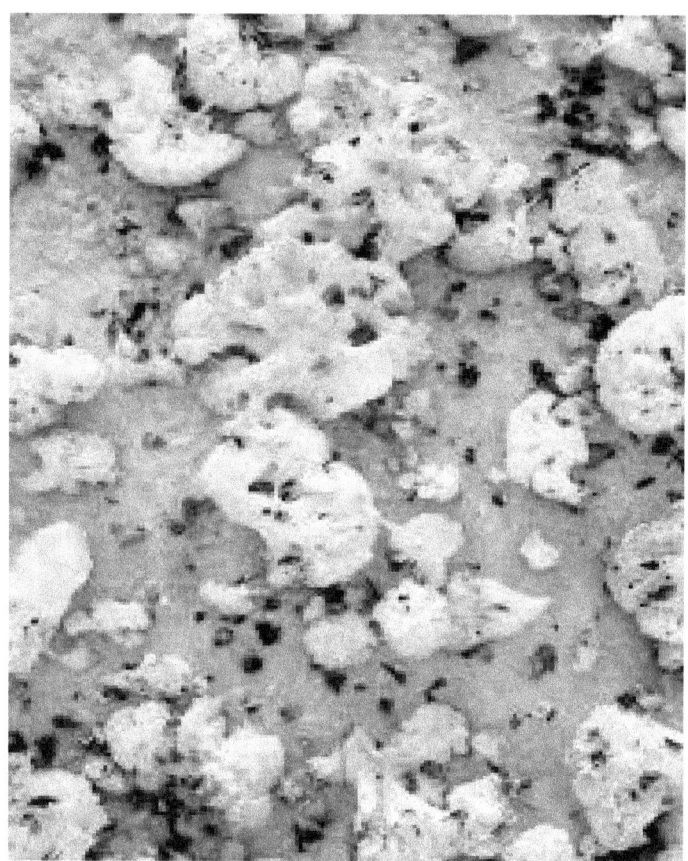

Preparation time: 10 Minutes

Cooking time: 25 Minutes

Servings: 6

Ingredients:

- 1 Cauliflower head, separated into florets
- Salt and ground black pepper, to taste
- ⅓ Cup Parmesan cheese, grated
- 1 Tablespoon fresh parsley, chopped

- 3 Tablespoons olive oil
- 2 Tablespoons extra virgin olive oil

Directions:

1. In a bowl, mix the oil with garlic, salt, pepper, and cauliflower florets.
2. Toss to coat well, spread this on a lined baking sheet, place in an oven at 450ºF, and bake for 25 minutes, stirring halfway.
3. Add the Parmesan cheese, and parsley, stir and cook for 5 minutes.
4. Divide between plates and serve.

Nutrition:

- Calories: 118
- Fat: 2g
- Fiber: 3g
- Carbohydrates: 2g
- Protein: 6g

Spicy Pecans

Preparation time: 10 Minutes

Cooking time: 3 Hours

Servings: 16

Ingredients:

- 3lbs. Pecan halves
- 2 Tbsp. Cajun seasoning blend
- 2 Tbsp. olive oil

Directions:

1. Add all ingredients to the slow cooker and stir well to combine.
2. Cover slow cooker with lid and cook on low for 1 hour.
3. Stir well. Cover again and cook for 2 hours more.
4. Serve and enjoy.

Nutrition:

- Calories: 607
- Fat: 62.5g
- Carbohydrates: 12.2g
- Sugar: 3g
- Protein: 9.1g
- Cholesterol: 0mg

Grilled Halloumi Cheese with Eggs

Preparation time: 15 Minutes

Cooking time: 10 Minutes

Servings: 4

Ingredients:

- 4 Slices halloumi cheese
- 3 Tsp. olive oil
- 1 Tsp. dried Greek seasoning blend
- 1 Tbsp. olive oil
- 6 Eggs, beaten
- 1/2 Tsp. sea salt

- 1/4 Tsp. crushed red pepper flakes
- 1 1/2 Cups avocado, pitted and sliced
- 1 Cup grape tomatoes, halved
- 4 Tbsp. pecans, chopped

Directions:

1. Preheat your grill to medium.
2. Set the Halloumi in the center of a piece of heavy-duty foil.
3. Sprinkle oil over the Halloumi and apply Greek seasoning blend.
4. Close the foil to create a packet.
5. Grill for about 15 minutes, then slice into four pieces.
6. In a frying pan, warm one tablespoon of oil and cook the eggs.
7. Stir well to create large and soft curds—season with salt and pepper.
8. Put the eggs and grilled cheese on a serving bowl.
9. Serve alongside tomatoes and avocado, decorated with chopped pecans.

Nutrition:

- Calories: 219
- Fat: 5.1g
- Fiber: 4.9g
- Carbohydrates: 1.5 g
- Protein: 3.9g

About the author

Dana Roberts is an author, nutritionist and mom of three beautiful princesses.
At the age of 38 she discovered that she had breast disease and this brought her a big hormonal imbalance.
At the age of 43 she noticed a gradual weight gain that prompted her to try different diets.
So many of these had little or no effect on her. After a few years, her body underwent drastic changes.
She gained a lot of weight, her breasts collapsed and a lot of stretch marks appeared. Not wanting to risk serious health problems, she discovered the ketogenic diet and decided to try it.
She began to notice that some foods gave her more energy and others weighed her down. Food addiction also influenced her diet because when she didn't bring awareness to her emotions, she reacted by eating.
She spent years fighting this addiction and finally found a way to overcome it and rediscover her former beauty, creating recipes that could fill both her stomach and her soul.
The book "Keto Diet Cookbook for women after 50" offers to all women the possibility to lose weight with a program based not only on diet, but also on the addiction that sometimes food creates.

CPSIA information can be obtained
at www.ICGtesting.com
Printed in the USA
BVHW041206270221
601119BV00023B/617